My Years to Remember

There is so much worth remembering...

The little surprises, the perfect days, the conversations that meant everything... the daily challenges and joys, the big decisions and the dreams come true. Every single year of your life, there are milestones to note, memories to capture, and moments worth holding on to.

This is a place to gather them all—each important piece. It's a place to celebrate what has been, to savor what's here now, and look forward to all that is coming.

...it is very important to be in love with life.

KEITH HARING

YEAR:

THIS IS MY ____ BIRTHDAY:

These are some events, milestones, and big moments from the last year that I'd like to remember...

These are some of my hopes, wishes, and plans for the year to come:

Reflections

These days, I am more deeply appreciating:

This is something I'm becoming newly interested in:

Lately, these are some of my favorite ways to spend my time:

In the coming year, I am curious to try:

Remembering the day

I celebrated my birthday this year by:

This is a wonderful day. I've never seen this one before.

MAYA ANGELOU

YEAR:

THIS IS MY ____ BIRTHDAY:

These are some events, milestones, and big moments from the last year that I'd like to remember...

These are some of my hopes, wishes, and plans for the year to come:

Reflections

Lately, I feel a lot of enthusiasm for:

Some routines or rituals I'm finding a lot of satisfaction in:

These are some positive changes that have happened in the past year:

Some new things I feel ready to try or begin include:

Remembering the day

I celebrated my birthday this year by:

...the world needs
your brilliance, your
voice, your unique
imagination, and
your particular genius.

GLORIA BURGESS

YEAR:

THIS IS MY ____ BIRTHDAY:

These are some events, milestones, and big moments from the last year that I'd like to remember...

These are some of my hopes, wishes, and plans for the year to come:

Reflections

Lately, I feel myself growing in my ability to:

I'm becoming more truly myself in these ways:

More than ever, I love:

Some dreams I am holding close right now:

Remembering the day

I celebrated my birthday this year by:

Each day become
more fully alive.

STEPHEN LEVINE

YEAR:

THIS IS MY ____ BIRTHDAY:

These are some events, milestones, and big moments from the last year that I'd like to remember...

These are some of my hopes, wishes, and plans for the year to come:

Reflections

Something I've recently learned or discovered about myself:

A skill I'm currently cultivating is:

One of my bravest moments in the past year was:

Lately, I feel most fully alive when:

Remembering the day

I celebrated my birthday this year by:

May the year to come
offer you more—more joy,
more laughter, more
wisdom, more growth,
more opportunity.

May you feel deeply
at home in the world;
may you find yourself right
where you're meant to be.

The biggest adventure you can ever take is to live the life of your dreams...

OPRAH WINFREY

YEAR:

THIS IS MY ____ BIRTHDAY:

These are some events, milestones, and big moments from the last year that I'd like to remember...

These are some of my hopes, wishes, and plans for the year to come:

Reflections

The person I was five years ago would be amazed that:

Something or someone I've been inspired by this year:

Lately, I'm proud of the way I:

Today, I want to promise myself that I will try:

Remembering the day

I celebrated my birthday this year by:

You change the world by being yourself.

YOKO ONO

YEAR:

THIS IS MY ____ BIRTHDAY:

These are some events, milestones, and big moments from the last year that I'd like to remember...

These are some of my hopes, wishes, and plans for the year to come:

Reflections

These days, I feel very fully like myself when I:

Lately, I'm prioritizing my well-being and happiness by:

I love that I'm the only person I know who:

I want to give myself credit and recognition for:

Remembering the day

I celebrated my birthday this year by:

Become the person you were meant to be… follow your heart's desire.

LEON BROWN

YEAR:

THIS IS MY ____ BIRTHDAY:

These are some events, milestones, and big moments from the last year that I'd like to remember...

These are some of my hopes, wishes, and plans for the year to come:

Reflections

I am learning to respect my own needs, wants, and preferences by:

I am becoming more and more capable of:

Something I'm glad I got to experience this year:

This birthday feels like a new beginning in this way:

Remembering the day

I celebrated my birthday this year by:

There are possibilities all around you...

KEKE PALMER

YEAR:

THIS IS MY ____ BIRTHDAY:

These are some events, milestones, and big moments from the last year that I'd like to remember...

These are some of my hopes, wishes, and plans for the year to come:

Reflections

Something I recently learned to make or do:

I appreciate that I'm becoming more and more comfortable with:

This year has given me the opportunity to:

In the year to come, I'm really looking forward to:

Remembering the day

I celebrated my birthday this year by:

May you remember
how deeply you matter
and how much of a
difference you make—
to the world around
you, to the people
who know you,
each and every day.

...each day
is a new
beginning...

CATHERINE PULSIFER

YEAR:

THIS IS MY ____ BIRTHDAY:

These are some events, milestones, and big moments from the last year that I'd like to remember...

These are some of my hopes, wishes, and plans for the year to come:

Reflections

Something new I'm learning these days is:

I'm making more room in my life for:

These are some patterns, aspects, or behaviors I'm letting go of:

I'm feeling a sense of optimism about:

Remembering the day

I celebrated my birthday this year by:

Perhaps this very instant is your time.

LOUISE BOGAN

YEAR:

THIS IS MY ____ BIRTHDAY:

These are some events, milestones, and big moments from the last year that I'd like to remember...

These are some of my hopes, wishes, and plans for the year to come:

Reflections

The person I was ten years ago would be so surprised to discover that:

These days, I'm finding a lot of meaning and purpose in:

I'm so grateful that at this stage in my life, I am:

Some of my life's most important work so far has been:

Remembering the day

I celebrated my birthday this year by:

The experience
of experiences
is being alive...

CARLOS CASTAÑEDA

YEAR:

THIS IS MY ____ BIRTHDAY:

These are some events, milestones, and big moments from the last year that I'd like to remember...

These are some of my hopes, wishes, and plans for the year to come:

Reflections

Something I've grown to love about myself is:

I feel incredibly fortunate to:

One of the biggest motivations in my life so far has been:

I think the coming year will be all about:

Remembering the day

I celebrated my birthday this year by:

Cherish
all your happy
moments...

BOOTH TARKINGTON

YEAR:

THIS IS MY ____ BIRTHDAY:

These are some events, milestones, and big moments from the last year that I'd like to remember...

These are some of my hopes, wishes, and plans for the year to come:

Reflections

A memory that feels particularly potent or meaningful lately:

A few favorite songs, meals, objects, and places from the past year:

Some people who feel deeply important to me right now:

Lately, the highlight of my days or weeks is:

Remembering the day

I celebrated my birthday this year by:

May you offer yourself
your own appreciation—
for everything you have
been, and everything
you have grown to be...
for all the ways the
years have revealed your
unique brilliance, your
profound capabilities.

...we all have the power
to make wishes come true...

LOUISA MAY ALCOTT

YEAR:

THIS IS MY ____ BIRTHDAY:

These are some events, milestones, and big moments from the last year that I'd like to remember...

These are some of my hopes, wishes, and plans for the year to come:

Reflections

It's taken me awhile, but I'm proud to say that:

I hope I am impacting the world for the better by:

My biggest wish right now is:

A word or theme I want to incorporate into this next year is:

Remembering the day

I celebrated my birthday this year by:

We turn not
older with years,
but newer
every day.

EMILY DICKINSON

YEAR:

THIS IS MY ____ BIRTHDAY:

These are some events, milestones, and big moments from the last year that I'd like to remember...

These are some of my hopes, wishes, and plans for the year to come:

Reflections

These are some of my favorite aspects of myself:

Some new things I'm trying lately include:

I am grateful to my younger self for:

I love that I am changing in these ways:

Remembering the day

I celebrated my birthday this year by:

We have to dare to be ourselves...

MAY SARTON

YEAR:

THIS IS MY ____ BIRTHDAY:

These are some events, milestones, and big moments from the last year that I'd like to remember...

These are some of my hopes, wishes, and plans for the year to come:

Reflections

The person I was fifteen years ago would love to know that:

The older I get, the more I cherish:

These are some things I know I will always love:

I'd like to start appreciating myself more often by:

Remembering the day

I celebrated my birthday this year by:

Each year is special and precious...

LOUISE HAY

YEAR:

THIS IS MY ____ BIRTHDAY:

These are some events, milestones, and big moments from the last year that I'd like to remember...

These are some of my hopes, wishes, and plans for the year to come:

Reflections

The best thing about the age I am is:

A challenge I met this year was:

Lately, I feel such gratitude for:

I am making extra time right now for:

Remembering the day

I celebrated my birthday this year by:

May today give you glimpses of all that's to come: the good things that are still in store... the wishes that are on their way to becoming true... and all the wonders that the world has yet to show you.

...a joyful life is made up of joyful moments...

BRENÉ BROWN

YEAR:

THIS IS MY ____ BIRTHDAY:

These are some events, milestones, and big moments from the last year that I'd like to remember...

These are some of my hopes, wishes, and plans for the year to come:

Reflections

I'm finding deep joy right now in:

I always feel good when I remember to:

I hope that I never outgrow my appreciation of:

Some things I want to do much more of:

Remembering the day

I celebrated my birthday this year by:

The most important thing is to enjoy your life...

AUDREY HEPBURN

YEAR:

THIS IS MY ____ BIRTHDAY:

These are some events, milestones, and big moments from the last year that I'd like to remember...

These are some of my hopes, wishes, and plans for the year to come:

Reflections

Some little things that mean a lot to me lately:

The moments I enjoy most are the ones I spend:

An important thing I'm coming to understand about myself is:

Something I want to learn or try in the year ahead:

Remembering the day

I celebrated my birthday this year by:

...savor the day
and be good
to yourself...

CHARLOTTE RAE

YEAR:

THIS IS MY ____ BIRTHDAY:

These are some events, milestones, and big moments from the last year that I'd like to remember...

____

____

____

____

____

____

These are some of my hopes, wishes, and plans for the year to come:

____

____

____

____

____

____

Reflections

I am honoring and taking good care of myself by:

These are some of the things I'm proudest of accomplishing:

I hope the people I love think of me as:

I feel one of a kind in the following ways:

Remembering the day

I celebrated my birthday this year by:

The longer
I live, the more
beautiful
life becomes.

FRANK LLOYD WRIGHT

YEAR:

THIS IS MY ____ BIRTHDAY:

These are some events, milestones, and big moments from the last year that I'd like to remember...

These are some of my hopes, wishes, and plans for the year to come:

Reflections

The person I was twenty years ago would be delighted to find that:

My life becomes fuller and more beautiful when I make sure to:

Some of the wisdom I'm grateful to have acquired through the years:

A few of the small wonders that make my world complete:

Remembering the day

I celebrated my birthday this year by:

May you delight in
the story of your life—
the pieces you've written
so far, and the pieces
you have yet to write.

May there be room
for everything you are
still becoming.

Two Decades of People and Places

These are some people who have supported me through the years, and the ways they made a difference:

NAME: ______________________________

They helped me by:

____

____

NAME: ______________________________

They helped me by:

____

____

NAME: ______________________________

They helped me by:

____

____

NAME: ______________________________

They helped me by:

____

____

These are some places that have shaped my last two decades, and why they're so important:

PLACE: ______

What it means to me:

______

______

PLACE: ______

What it means to me:

______

______

PLACE: ______

What it means to me:

______

______

PLACE: ______

What it means to me:

______

______

Two Decades of Being

Looking back over the last twenty years, these are some of the ways I have stayed very much the same:

These are some of the ways I've changed:

These are some of the greatest joys I got to experience:

These are some of the challenges that grew me and shaped me:

A Moment to Look Forward

Some new things I am looking forward to doing, trying, and exploring:

Personal goals I want to accomplish:

Important things I want to make more time for:

These are some of the biggest dreams I have for the future:

COMPENDIUM®
live inspired

Written and compiled by: M.H. Clark
Designed by: Jessica Phoenix
Edited by: Miriam Hathaway

ISBN: 978-1-957891-41-5

1st printing. Printed in China with soy inks on FSC®-Mix certified paper.

Create meaningful moments with gifts that inspire.

CONNECT WITH US
live-inspired.com | sayhello@compendiuminc.com

@compendiumliveinspired
#compendiumliveinspired